# Minstrels

## medieval music to sing and play

selected and edited by

BRIAN SARGENT

*Keswick Hall College of Education, Norwich*

CAMBRIDGE UNIVERSITY PRESS

# The Resources of Music Series

General Editors: *Wilfrid Mellers, John Paynter*

1. THE RESOURCES OF MUSIC *by Wilfrid Mellers*
2. SOUND AND SILENCE *by John Paynter and Peter Aston*
3. SOMETHING TO PLAY *by Geoffrey Brace*
4. MUSIC DRAMA IN SCHOOLS *edited by Malcolm John*
5. THE PAINFUL PLOUGH *by Roy Palmer*
6. THE VALIANT SAILOR *by Roy Palmer*
7. TROUBADOURS *by Brian Sargent*
8. MINSTRELS *by Brian Sargent*
9. POVERTY KNOCK *by Roy Palmer*

# Acknowledgements

Full source references to songs and prose passages are given on page 48. Sources of illustrations are listed on page 48. The author and publisher would like to thank all those there listed for permission to reproduce material in this book.

While every effort has been made to contact copyright holders, the publishers apologise if any material has been included without permission.

Performing and recording rights are reserved and are administered by the Performing Rights Society, The Mechanical Copyright Protection Society and the affiliated bodies throughout the world. Applications should be made to these bodies for a relevant licence. Failure to so apply constitutes a breach of copyright.

*Front cover: A medieval bagpipe player. The musicians on the title page are playing cymbals. Both illustrations are from a thirteenth-century Spanish manuscript.*

CAMBRIDGE UNIVERSITY PRESS
Cambridge, New York, Melbourne, Madrid, Cape Town,
Singapore, São Paulo, Delhi, Tokyo, Mexico City

Cambridge University Press
The Edinburgh Building, Cambridge CB2 8RU, UK

Published in the United States of America by Cambridge University Press, New York

www.cambridge.org
Information on this title: www.cambridge.org/9780521201667

© Cambridge University Press 1974

This publication is in copyright. Subject to statutory exception and to the provisions of relevant collective licensing agreements, no reproduction of any part may take place without the written permission of Cambridge University Press.

First published 1974
Re-issued 2011

*A catalogue record for this publication is available from the British Library*

*Library of Congress Catalogue Card Number: 73-80470*

ISBN 978-0-521-20166-7 Paperback

Cambridge University Press has no responsibility for the persistence or accuracy of URLs for external or third-party internet websites referred to in this publication, and does not guarantee that any content on such websites is, or will remain, accurate or appropriate.

# Contents

**Introduction** page 4

**Excerpts from plays**

1. Danielis ludus (The Play of Daniel) — 8
2. Li Gieus de Robin et de Marion (Robin and Marion) by Adam de la Halle — 14
3. The Spicers' Play and the carol, Nova, nova — 19

**Part songs**

4. (a) Nobilis, humilis (Mighty Lord) — 24
4. (b) Edi beo thu (Heav'nly Queen/Welcome) — 26
5. Ad cantus laetitiae (Under Bethlem's star) — 28
6. (a) Alleluia — 29
6. (b) Rosa fragrans (Keep us all) — 30
7. Ave mater Domini (Harvest time is here) by Walter Odington — 31
8. Talent m'est pris (Now is the time) — 32
9. (a) Hey, Robyn (Robin, hey!) by William Cornyshe — 34
9. (b) Martinslied (Worthy friends, good evening!) — 35

**Instrumental music**

10. (a) Danse royale (*Ductia*) (Court dance) — 37
10. (b) Ich spring an disem ringe (I jump into this ring) — 38
11. (a) Cauda (Tail-piece) — 38
11. (b) Amor potest (Love can complain) — 40
12. Dit le bourguignon (The Burgundian speaks) — 43

**Suggestions for further activities** — 46

**Sources** — 48

# Introduction

Over the past few years there have been signs of an increasing interest in medieval music. Recitals of attractive and colourful examples from the period are now quite common, and numerous ensembles have been formed for their performance. The number of people for whom the expression 'medieval music' conjures up the prospect of a dreary and forbidding mystery is steadily diminishing.

In the field of so-called 'educational music' the pioneer work of Ralph Dunstan and Christopher Bygott in *Musical appreciation through song* (Schofield & Sims, 1922), which incorporated several examples of medieval music, was, as far as I know, alone until relatively recently. Now, however, one may see evidence of the growing interest in music of this period in recent publications and also for example in BBC music programmes for schools. Even so, some of its potentialities for school use remain untapped, and this book is an attempt to remedy the neglect.

It is all too easy to forget that what we sometimes casually call medieval music can cover a vast stretch of some 600 years, from approximately the beginning of the ninth century to at least the end of the fourteenth, in other words, a period longer than that from AD 1400 to the present day. If one thinks of the developments which have taken place since about 1400 it is easy to realize what a vast and varied quantity of medieval music must still exist, even making allowance for a generally slower rate of change and for a high mortality rate among manuscripts. A Goliard song and a Machaut chanson may differ as profoundly as a Bach aria and a Wolf Lied. But such immense variety is clearly a strong advantage, and one which will be appreciated more and more as a greater familiarity with the music of those times develops.

## Texts

Of course the resurrection of such music for workaday use by ordinary people is not without its problems. Chief of these is the provision of suitable words. Existing texts are either in Latin, langue d'oc (Provençal), langue d'oïl (medieval French), Middle High German or Middle English. The subject matter of most of the songs is love, whether courtly, romantic or sexual, and much of the imagery precious and whimsical. Although nowadays the experts tell us that schoolboys' supposed traditional distaste for love songs and references to sweet maids, singing birds, babbling brooks, moonlight and roses is largely a myth (and certainly, few pop song texts – admittedly more down to earth – seem to offend), even so, there must be a limit to their tolerance. Another problem is posed by the uncomfortably high proportion of medieval song texts pouring lavish praise on the Virgin Mary. In this book a variety of solutions is offered; in some cases existing verse translations have, with permission, been used; in others new unrelated 'poems' in various styles have been provided, and sometimes the original text has been kept in the hope of encouraging people who use the book either to attempt medieval pronunciation occasionally or to create suitable texts of their own. In this connection it is a comfort to remember that much medieval song verse is, to put it mildly, hardly top-class poetry, and also that in the Middle Ages folk were much less rigid than we are in discriminating between the sacred and the secular. Some of the latter songs, for example, the Goliard song *O admirabile Veneris idolum* and the famous *Sumer* canon, are furnished with alternative sacred texts, some are based on plainsong material, and some sacred motets contain overtly secular melodies.

In strophic songs, the words of the first stanza have been placed under the notes of the melody. Although this is the most practical course, it has been taken with some reluctance as there is a risk that the other stanzas may then tend to be neglected. It is hoped that this will not be the case, as the words of all the stanzas should fit their respective melodies equally well.

## Rhythm

Another problem, and one which diminishes with the later forms of medieval notation, is that of the rhythm of the music. For example, many of the monodic (solo) songs of medieval times survive only in manuscripts which, though reasonably clear as to pitch, give little or no indication of the intended rhythm. Writing as recently as 1973, Gilbert Reaney says, 'We continue to be uncertain about the rhythm of plainsong and Troubadour song and about how to perform the lower parts of medieval motets and polyphonic songs' (*Soundings* 3, University College Cardiff). The most generally accepted solution is to apply to the melodic outline the note values of the rhythmic mode which corresponds with the poetic metre of the text to which the music is set. According, therefore, to the metre of the text concerned, the rhythm of the song may be trochaic: ♩ ♪♪ ♩ etc. (mode 1), as in No. 11a and many others; iambic: ♪♩ ♪♩ etc. (mode 2); dactylic: ♩. ♪♪ etc. (mode 3); anapaestic: ♪♪ ♩. etc. (mode 4); spondaic: ♩. ♩. etc. (mode 5); or even tribrachic: ♪♪♪ etc. (mode 6). Although, as will be seen, this practice generally leads to unrelieved 6/8 time, some authorities believe that mode 3 may be transcribed in 2/4 time (♩ ♪♪) and mode 5 in 4/4 (♩♩ etc.), so a certain amount of variety is possible.

### Pitch

As regards pitch, it is fortunate that many of the song melodies of this period are of limited compass and therefore quite easily adaptable to any range of voice. As such songs may be accompanied by unpitched percussion only, with an occasional drone, there need be no problems involved in transposition. If recorders or other melody instruments are used it will be advisable to consider the technical implications before deciding on transposition to another key. Medieval melodies were originally written in C clef notation, and modern transcriptions use either the ordinary treble clef or the treble clef with an 'octave lower' sign, thus 𝄞. In order to avoid confusion the former is taken as standard when comparing the original pitch of the tunes with the pitch used here.

### Interpretation

One of the greatest advantages of the music of this time is the variety of differing treatments which it will accept. Such music will tolerate a great deal of experiment in the manner of its performance, and widely divergent interpretations may often be regarded – with little fear of contradiction – as reasonably authentic.

Here are a few suggestions for the varied treatment of pieces in this book and elsewhere. Some of the songs will be found to be designed for solo and chorus treatment; these and perhaps others may be performed antiphonally by groups of similar or differing size. Some gain by the doubling of the melody line at the unison or octave by instruments such as recorders, or by voices or instruments at the interval of a fourth below or fifth above. Pedals or drones, single or double (a fifth apart) may sometimes be added where suitable instruments are available – and where, of course, the nature of the melody permits. Introductions, interludes and codas for instruments may be derived from the melodic material of the song, this at its humblest level involving no more than the use of the first or last phrase of the melody. Simple parts for unpitched percussion instruments may be devised in most cases. These may either mark the basic pulse, pick out the prevailing rhythmic mode or, occasionally perhaps, provide a contrasting rhythm. Experiment, and let the ear decide which result is musically the most satisfactory.

### Instrumentation

Although it seems unlikely that instruments other than organ and bells were officially sanctioned for use in the church service there was certainly a wide variety available elsewhere. A good reference book on the subject (for example, Anthony Baines, *Musical instruments through the ages*, Pelican, 1961, ch. 9) will provide much more information than there is room to give here. However, some brief mention of these instruments is necessary so that the most suitable modern substitutes may be selected. The groups most likely to have been involved in medieval times are:

(a) plucked and struck string (citole, gittern, harp, lute, lyre, psaltery);

*Organistrum*

*Chimebells*

*Musicians, from a thirteenth-century Spanish MS*

*Sixteenth-century musicians playing pipe and tabor, trumpet, harp and dulcimer*

only all too rare in many schools even now; they are also, particularly in the case of the former, too smooth in tone to provide realistic substitutes for their medieval counterparts – though here again the rougher tone of a student may be a help rather than a hindrance! The sound of the humble melodica, though rather dull and soon likely to pall, may be pressed into service if necessary. Or if really hard up, but equipped with a competent trumpeter, one might experiment with various kinds of mute. The smooth tone of the single-reed clarinet, though readily available among present-day amateurs, seems less appropriate to our notions of medieval sound, but there are those who believe that its tone may not be unlike that of the mysterious douçaine.

Recorders in their various sizes are the automatic representatives of group (d). It is worth taking some trouble over the balance of these instruments; for example, one may discover that in certain conditions the shrill clarity of a plastic descant will balance a combination of two softer-toned wooden descants, or a wooden descant and tenor played in octaves.

If a pipe, reed or even electronic organ should happen to be available, it is worth remembering that the tiny medieval portative organ was, as often as not, a secular melodic instrument, its function very different from that of the organ in more recent times.

Bass instruments for pedals and drones (don't overwork the drones!) will in all probability choose themselves, a 'cello or viola being by far the most suitable, though a trombone or bassoon (or even a convenient brass band instrument) might successfully play a tenor part, as in No. 11b.

Of the pitched percussion instruments, the glockenspiel is much more suitable than the xylophone, metallophone or chime bars. Tunable tambours can represent nakers.

There is great variety in the field of unpitched percussion, but naturally some types of instrument are more appropriate than others. Small drums, tambourines, triangles and 'Indian' cymbals can all play a useful part. It is advisable to be careful in the choice of drum; some emit a sound of unmistakable pitch which can be distinctly uncomfortable if it is at variance with the tonality of the music.

In most of the pieces a choice of percussion rhythms is suggested, varied to suit the pace at which you decide the music shall move. Of course these rhythms may be combined if you wish, but make sure that the contribution of the percussion department is neither too heavy nor inflexible. The weaker beats should be played lightly, and singers should almost always heavily outnumber percussion players.

(b) bowed string (crowd [ =crwth], hurdy-gurdy, rebec, vièle);
(c) double-reed wind (bagpipe, shawm, and later, cornamuse and crumhorn);
(d) fipple wind (gemshorn, pipe (with tabor), recorder).

The obvious present-day substitute for group (a) is the guitar, which may be used purely for the melodic line, or as a harmony instrument providing suitable strummed chords (generally of the 'open fifth' type, that is, without the third of the chord present) on the strong beats (or some of them) and perhaps an introduction and/or interlude.

There can be no doubt, either, of the instruments for group (b). Because some parts (for example, the lower part of No. 4b and the lowest of No. 11b) are technically very simple, involving in some cases no more than three different notes, there may be an opportunity here for a relative beginner on the violin; his nasal tone may be nearer to that of a rebec than that of a more accomplished violinist! Moreover, if the part should be no more than a matter of open strings and first finger, the intonation may well be acceptable too. Or perhaps the competent player may experiment in playing nearer than usual to the bridge of his instrument.

Oboe and bassoon, the standard double-reed instruments of the present day, are not

Don't despise the humblest but most readily available forms of percussion: hand clapping, finger snapping, foot stamping and so on, where these are appropriate – and in no danger of disturbing occupants of the next room!

Those with a limited or non-existent piano technique will be relieved to discover that in this book there is no call whatever for the piano, which is one of the relatively few instruments which can have no place at all in the medieval musical scene. It would make a poor substitute even for a psaltery; give it a well-earned rest!

The chief object in scoring medieval music should be the selection of clear, bright, unequivocal colours (well contrasted in polyphonic textures), not necessarily crude or strident, but devoid of that smooth sophistication which one finds in the expressive playing of a modern oboist, or the lush vibrato of a skilled violinist.

**Tempi and expression**
The pace of these pieces is of course conjectural and subject to individual taste; the metronome markings provided should be regarded as no more than tentative suggestions. Try over the pieces at different speeds until you find your ideal. No expression marks have been added; this does not mean that the expression should be neglected, but that your own should evolve as your acquaintance with the pieces develops.

**Conclusion**
One final plea: don't give up if you can't achieve what you feel to be authentic results; it's far better to play an estampie on flute and clarinet or a motet on violin, melodica and horn, and to help matters along with a generous allowance of imagination, than to close the door on centuries of music for want of a rebec, a shawm or a psaltery. And after all, however much the scholars may debate, the sounds of recorders and human voices can't have changed so very much.

This collection is intended to open a door, to stimulate ideas and to encourage a search for further suitable material of this period. The music may at first seem a little strange,

*Angel blowing a trumpet –*
*from a thirteenth-century MS*

but it would be a great pity to let yourself be daunted by that as all the pieces have already been tried out in 'ordinary' schools under normal conditions. The first step is that of experiment, along the lines suggested above, in the matter of interpretation. The second concerns texts. If the mixture of originals, translations, paraphrases and independent compositions provided here doesn't meet with approval in certain circumstances, as may well be the case at times, please don't abandon all intention of using the music; try writing a text of your own. Sit down with a pencil, a sheet of blank paper and an open mind, and see what happens. You may be pleasantly surprised! For the third, a list of sources is given to assist those who have the interest and initiative to seek out further attractive pieces for themselves. The opportunities are great for those prepared to make the effort.

# Excerpts from plays

## 1 *Danielis ludus*

As early as the ninth century small fragments of dramatic dialogue had found their way into the church service. A well-known example from the tenth century represents the conversation between the angel and the women at the tomb of Jesus on Easter morning. By the twelfth century elaborate and often attractive plays were being performed – and still in church. Many of them originated in France, like the most famous of all, this Play of Daniel, though the text was in Latin. There is a lot of doubt and discussion as to which instruments were used in the performance of these plays. Some scholars favour a colourful profusion of string, wind and percussion instruments, while others assert that as the dramas were part of the church service, no more than organ and bells were permitted. But unless we intend to make our performances as authentic as possible we need not be unduly anxious over these scholarly issues.

Here is a part of the Play of Daniel, so adapted as to combine spoken dialogue and three chorus movements, one of which is used as an instrumental piece.

*Sculpture of Daniel in the lions' den, on the west front of Lincoln Cathedral*

**Speaking characters:**

Narrator  Belshazzar
The Queen  Daniel
An Astrologer  Chorus of Courtiers and Soldiers

Simple stage directions may be evolved to suit the situation.
Percussion parts and introductory instrumental phrases for the choruses may be fabricated if you wish. In 1C, Roman numerals at the beginnings of phrases of the music refer to the suggested antiphonal groups of musicians.

# *The Play of Daniel (excerpt)*

## 1a

**Introductory procession**
*Entry of the players*
(Plan of performance: A: group I, repeat group II; B: ditto; C: ditto; D (three times): I, II and I; C: II, repeat I; B: ditto; C: II, repeat I & II together.)

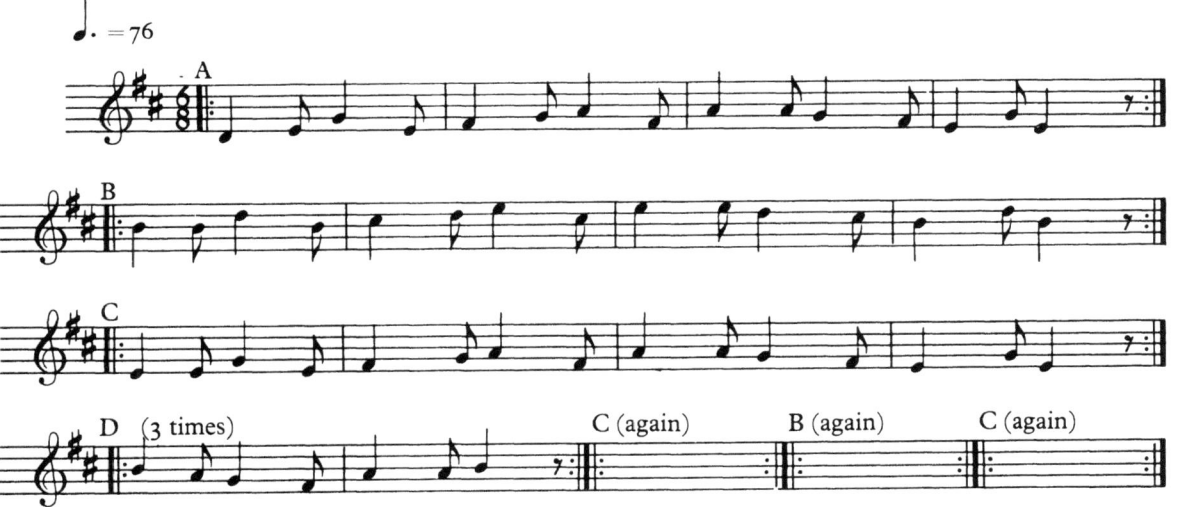

NARRATOR:  Mighty Belshazzar commands a feast;
A thousand lords give him thanks and glory.
Flushed and foolish, flown with pride,
He bids his servants bring hither
The goodly goblets of gold and silver,
The consecrated cups and vessels
Set aside for sacred use
In Jehovah's temple, but taken thence
When Nebuchadnezzar annexed Judah.
His wanton wives drink wine therefrom.
With lustful lips and looks profane,
Their shouts grow shameless at Belshazzar's table
In honour of idols of their own devising,
Forgetting God from whom all greatness comes.

ALL (*shouting*): Long live the King!

BELSHAZZAR: You who obey my voice,
Bring those vessels for my use
Which my father brought from the temple
When he severely crushed Judaea.

# 1b

*Processional chorus of the vessel-bearers (courtiers):*

I  Let us praise our noble monarch Mighty and victorious!
II Let his throng of merry subjects Glad allegiance render,

Let us with our joyful singing Make his name more glorious!
Play their harps or clap with spirit, Honour their defender.

I  Judah's temple was destroyed By his sire sagacious;
Now the son reigns in succession, equally tenacious.

II Sacred cups the former captured from the Jewish nation;
I & II So the latter feasts more grandly By this desecration.

I  Taken from Jerusalem, These, the vessels royal
II They to great Belshazzar come, Offering in duty

Babylon are now traversing, Borne by subjects loyal.
And respect to their great leader, Objects of such beauty.

NARRATOR: In this heedless hour a hand appears,
Phantom fingers come forth and write
Words on the wall, a wonder to behold.
The sight silences; they cease laughing;
Full of fear is the face of the King,
Belshazzar of Babylon; his bowels quake,
His knees knock. In his need he cries:

BELSHAZZAR: Call forth the Chaldaean astrologers
And the diviners;
Search out the soothsayers,
And bring forth the wise men.

*Optional instrumental interlude* (No. 10a or part of No. 1b)

*Entry of the Astrologers*

| | |
|---|---|
| AN ASTROLOGER: | Long live the King! |
| | Behold, we are here before you. |
| BELSHAZZAR: | Whoever reads this writing |
| | And unfolds its meaning |
| | Shall be given power over Babylon, |
| | And arrayed in purple |
| | Shall wear a golden collar. |
| ASTROLOGER: | We cannot solve the writing, nor give a clue |
| | As to what is written, nor find the meaning of the hand. |
| QUEEN: | Long live the King! |
| | That you may know the meaning of the writing, |
| | King Belshazzar, listen to this counsel. |
| | Together with the captives of Judaea |
| | One Daniel, learned in prophetic oracles, |
| | Was brought here, far from his home, |
| | Captured in your father's victory. |
| | Since he lives now under your rule, |
| | Reason demands he be summoned here. |
| | Command at once; let there be no delay, |
| | For he will explain what the vision conceals. |
| BELSHAZZAR: | |
| *(to his courtiers)* | Go you to seek out Daniel; |
| | Find him and bring him here. |

*Instrumental interlude* (as before) culminating in the return of the courtiers with Daniel:

| | |
|---|---|
| DANIEL: | Long live the King! |
| BELSHAZZAR: | Are you not called Daniel, |
| | Brought here with the wretches of Judaea? |
| | They say you have the spirit of God |
| | And foresee whatever is hidden. |
| | If then you can solve this writing, |
| | You will be enriched with countless gifts. |
| DANIEL: | O King, I wish not your gifts; |
| | Unrewarded I will solve the letters. |
| | This is the solution: Affliction awaits you. |
| | Your father above all others once was powerful. |
| | Swollen with excessive pride |
| | He was cast down from glory. |
| | For, not walking with God, |
| | But making of himself a god, |
| | He stole the vessels of the Temple |
| | And put them to his own use. |
| | But after many such mad deeds |
| | At the end he lost his wealth, |
| | And, deprived of human form, |
| | He fed on repasts of grass. |
| | And you, his son, as well, |
| | No less wicked than he, |
| | In following his example, |
| | Use these very same vessels. |
| | Since this is displeasing to God, |
| | The time of His vengeance is at hand, |
| | For the meaning of the writing |
| | Is to warn of retribution. |
| | For MENE, says the Lord, |
| | Is the end of your kingdom; |

TEKEL means a measuring weight,
Which means you are weaker;
PERES, that is division,
Your kingdom will be given to another.

BELSHAZZAR: Let him who has solved the secret
Be adorned with regal robes.
Take away the vessels, prince of my troops,
Lest they be the cause of misfortune to me.

# 1C

*Recessional march and chorus of soldiers:*

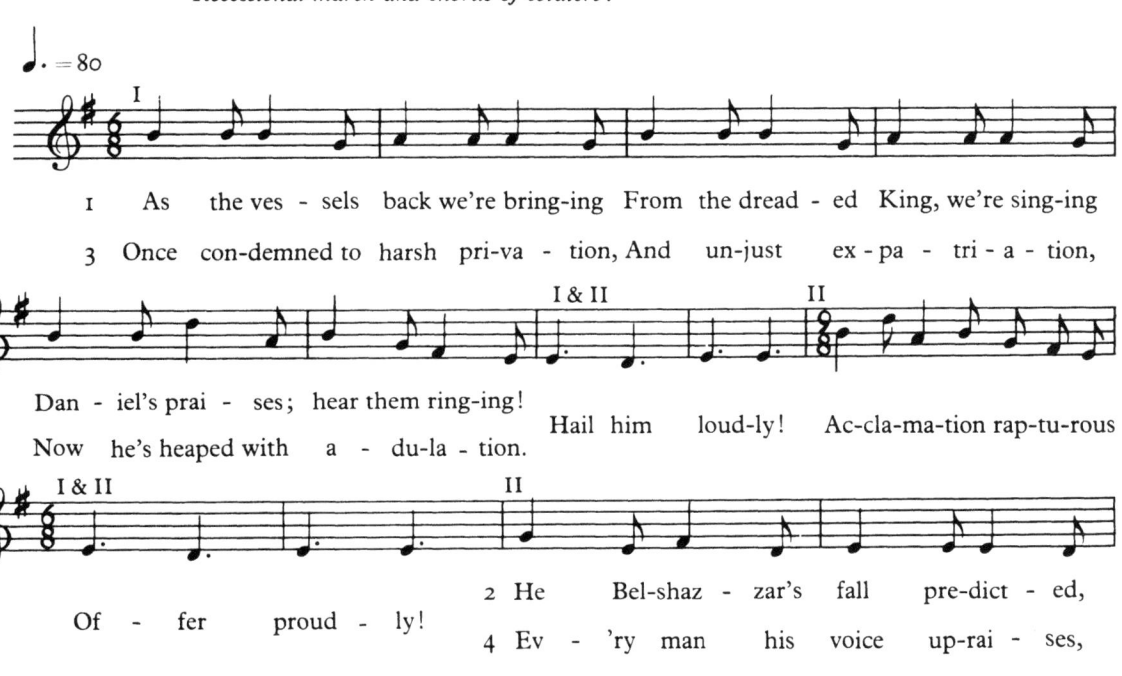

1 As the ves-sels back we're bring-ing From the dread-ed King, we're sing-ing
3 Once con-demned to harsh pri-va-tion, And un-just ex-pa-tri-a-tion,

Dan-iel's prai-ses; hear them ring-ing! Hail him loud-ly! Ac-cla-ma-tion rap-tu-rous
Now he's heaped with a-du-la-tion.

Of-fer proud-ly! 2 He Bel-shaz-zar's fall pre-dict-ed,
4 Ev-'ry man his voice up-rai-ses,

What the writ-ing meant de-pict-ed; False ac-cu-sers he con-vict-ed,
And in ad-mir-a-tion ga-zes. Far and wide his glo-ry bla-zes;

Freed Su-san-na much af-flict-ed. Hail him loud-ly!
E-ven Gen-tiles sing his prai-ses.

Ac-clam-a-tion rap-tu-rous Of-fer proud-ly! proud-ly!

# 2 Li Gieus de Robin et de Marion

This pastoral play with songs by Adam de la Halle is thought to have been written for the French court at Naples in about 1285. The song tunes may well have been popular melodies of the time, like those in *The Beggar's Opera* nearly 450 years later.

Simple stage directions for this excerpt may be worked out according to taste and the needs and opportunities of the situation. The *Danse royale* (No. 10a) may be used as an introduction. A suggested arrangement is given below. Instrumental introductions and percussion parts for the songs may be fabricated as required.

**Characters:** MARION, a shepherdess and
PERONNELLE (PENNY), her girl friend,
ROBIN, Marion's boy friend,
GAUTIER and BAUDON (WALTER and BALDWIN, his cousins,
HUART (HUGH), his friend, and two musicians.

In this excerpt, a Knight, Sir Aubert, does not appear, nor does Baudon speak. Baudon may be retained as a non-speaking part or perhaps replaced by a girl to provide balance in the dances. As an English text is being used the players may wish to substitute the English names given here or any others they may prefer.

*Adam de la Halle*

# The play of Robin and Marion (excerpt)

**Introduction:** *Danse royale* (No. 10a in the higher key)

HUGH: ... now we'll spread the picnic. What have you got tucked away here, Penny?

PENNY: That's bread, and here's salt and watercress. And you, Marion?

MARION: See what Robin has; for I've only a little cheese left over from this morning, and some bread, and these apples he brought me.

WALTER: Even if you don't want me as a boy friend, Penny, you won't turn up your nose at this smoked ham.

HUGH: Ham! You brought some ham?

WALTER: Indeed I have – there.

PENNY: And here are two fresh cheeses.

HUGH: Cow's milk or ewe's?

PENNY: Cheese from my own ewes.

HUGH: What can you give us, Robin?

ROBIN: Here's some cold pease pudding.

HUGH: Pease pudding! Is that all?

ROBIN: Poor man's goose – we can't all be as rich as Walter.

MARION: And nothing else, Robin?

ROBIN: Yes, there is something more – but you'll never guess, Marion.

MARION: Tell me, Robin, please.

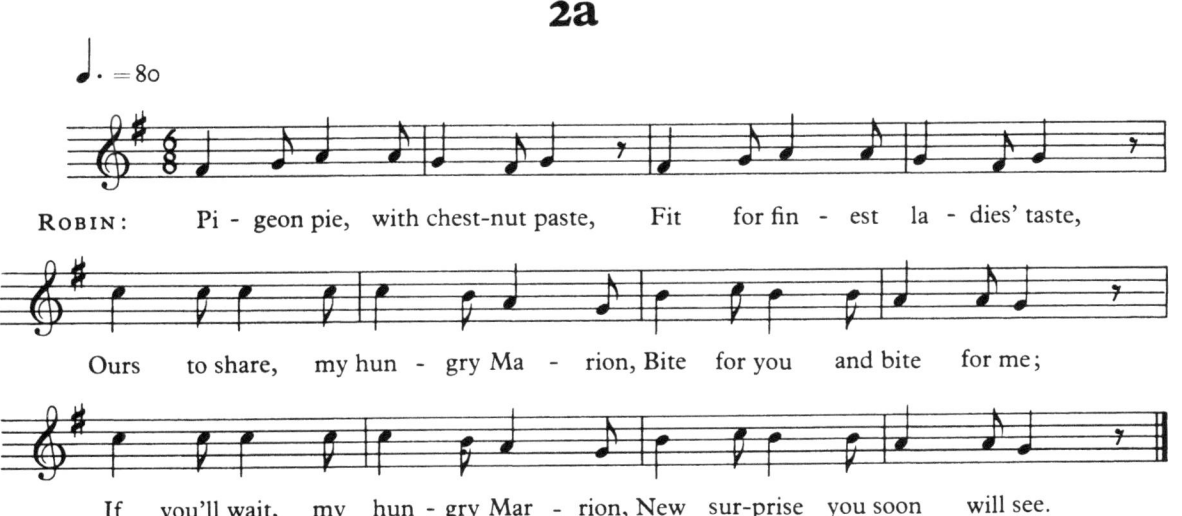

MARION: Pigeon pie! Oh, Robin, go on –

ROBIN: 2 Portly capon, crammed with meal, Bacon larded, and this we'll
Share together, hungry Marion, Bite for you and bite for me;
And we'll have some music, Marion, If you'll wait here patiently.

MARION: Robin, come back! Come back and join us!
ROBIN: I'll be back, darling. Start getting the feast ready, and I won't be long.
MARION: No, Robin, don't go; please come and sit down with us.
ROBIN: Be patient, my little Marion! Here, your skirt will do for a cloth; spread out the food, and I'll soon be with you again.
MARION: A white skirt, I think – yours, Penny – spread it just here.
PENNY: Hold my belt, Hugh. There, that'll do – and now you can see my smartest petticoat.
HUGH: Now, friends, we'll set the table: the bread, Penny's cheese, apples, pasty, pie. Look, I'll lift the crust: meat and jelly, egg, onion – and ah, the ham. And now here's Robin back.
MARION: And dancing as he comes!
PENNY: Now you see why he left us, Marion.
MARION: He's been to fetch – why, who are they? Do you know them, Walter?
WALTER: I don't know them, but I can see what they're carrying; they're musicians.
ROBIN: There, my sweetheart, I wasn't long, just long enough to wonder if you're still fond of me.

*Picture of Sir Aubert and Marion from the manuscript of the play*

MARION: And long enough for me to be sure that I am. But who are these two?

ROBIN: Musicians – I found them in the village. Listen, now, and we'll dance to their playing. Which one will you have? I'm good at them all, as you very well know!

MARION: Now, Robin, follow my leader.
ROBIN: Ah, that's better! Now I'll lead you a real dance. Are you all ready?
MARION: Take hands then, and follow. Give me your hand, Robin; now, Walter, you take mine, then Penny, then you, Hugh, and then *.
ROBIN: Off we go, then.

## 2c

ROB. Come follow me, follow me, follow.
ALL We follow, we follow, we follow,

ROB. Wend your way toward the greenwood; follow onward merrily.
ALL Wend our way toward the greenwood, and we follow merrily.

* Baldwin, or any other boy's or girl's name.

# 3 *The Spicers' Play* and the carol, *Nova, nova*

Mystery plays were a vivid feature of life in the late Middle Ages. They were not thrillers or 'Whodunits' but fascinating dramatizations of Bible stories for the benefit of the ordinary folk, most of whom could neither read nor write. They were arranged in a series or cycle, covering the main Biblical stories from the Creation to the Last Judgement, and each play was the responsibility of a particular guild of tradesmen, the Carpenters' Guild, for example, the Locksmiths' or the Tailors'.

Mystery plays from Chester, Coventry, Wakefield and other cities survive; this excerpt is from the York cycle. It was written some time between 1350 and 1430, possibly by a monk or monks of St Mary's Abbey in York. Originally there were no less than fifty-seven plays (forty-eight now survive), and for about 200 years they were performed on the feast of Corpus Christi (the Thursday after Trinity Sunday), a public holiday in May or June. On the eve of Corpus Christi the town crier read a proclamation which instructed all citizens to go unarmed and all guilds to have their plays ready for the following day. Each play was enacted on a pageant waggon at twelve different places in the city, and the complete performance ran from 4.30 in the morning until dusk.

Performance of the plays was discontinued about 1570 and was revived for the occasion of the York Festival in Festival of Britain Year, 1951. Since then the plays have been performed in St Mary's Abbey grounds at intervals of about three years, and have proved as absorbing in the twentieth century as they seem to have been in the fifteenth. Needless to say, the modern performances are much shorter than their medieval counterparts!

Carols were originally dance songs, but by the fifteenth century they had lost their direct association with dancing and had become songs (generally lively and rhythmic) in celebration of a festival or season, for example, Christmas, Easter, spring or harvest. They were generally in the form: burden (a kind of refrain), stanza, burden, stanza, burden, etc., always beginning and ending with the burden.

The carol *Nova, nova* may be used to introduce or conclude the Spicers' Play, or its stanzas, each with its own burden (see note, p. 23), may be interspersed among the speeches in the dialogue between Gabriel and Mary.

It seems likely that in medieval times the plainsong Magnificat (Mary's song of praise to God) was sung during the course of the play.

*Fourteenth-century mummers*

# The Spicers' Play

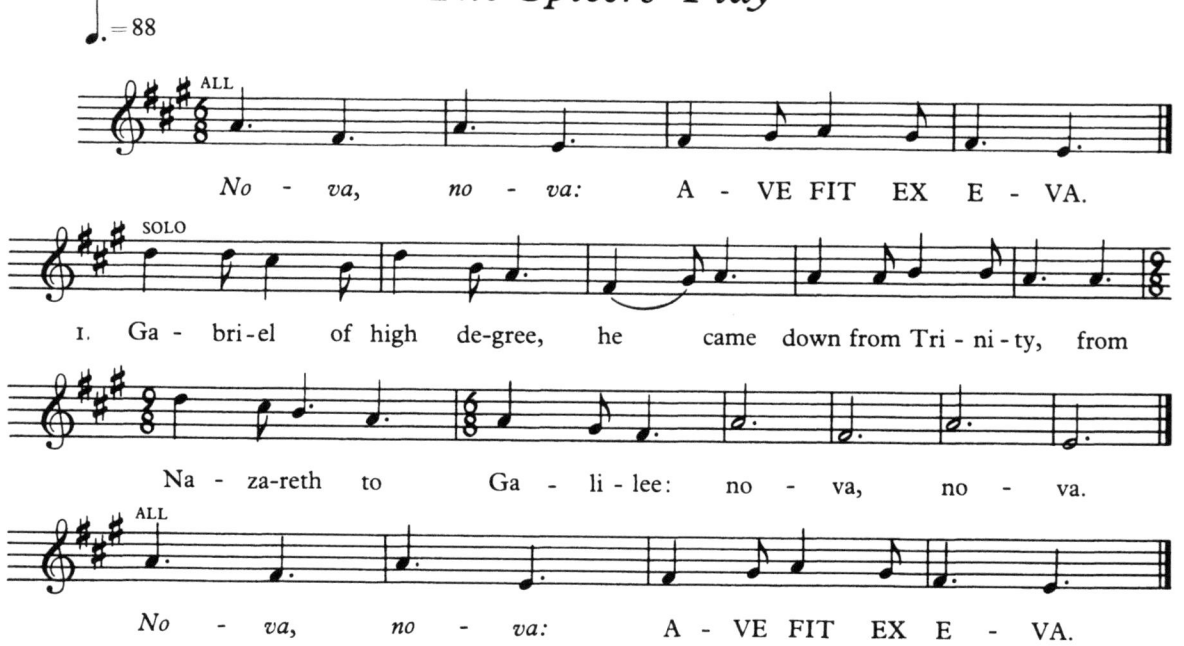

ANGEL: Hail, Mary, full of grace and bliss,
Our Lord God is with thee,
And hath chosen thee for his;
Of all women blest might thou be.

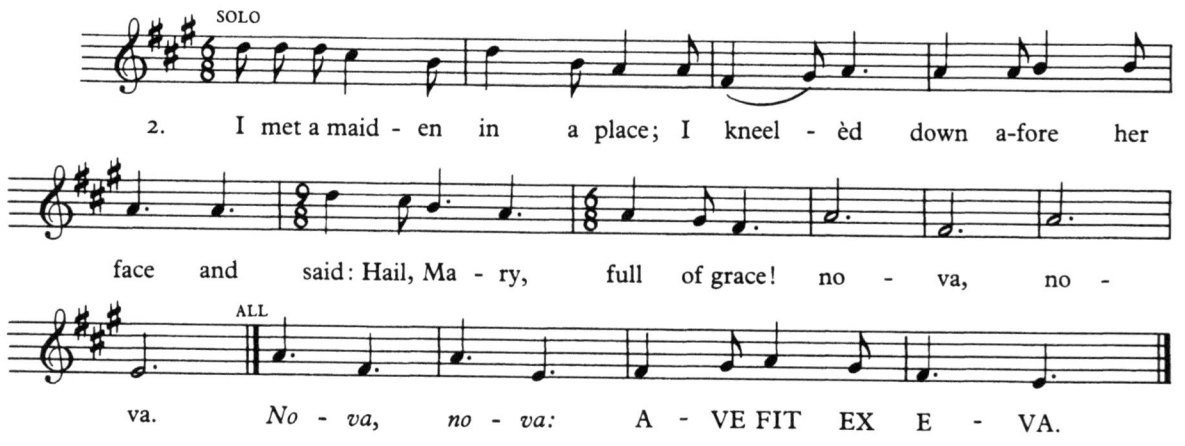

MARY: What manner of hailing is this,
That privily comes to me?
For in my heart a thought there is –
What is this tokening that I see?

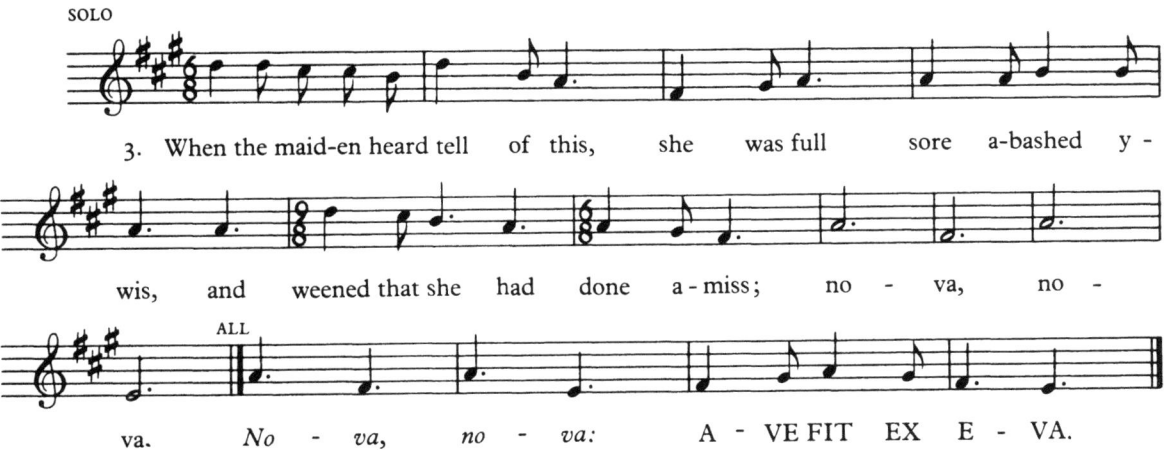

3. When the maiden heard tell of this, she was full sore abashed ywis, and weened that she had done amiss; no-va, no-va. Nova, nova: AVE FIT EX EVA.

ANGEL: Now dread thou nought, thou mild Mary,
For nothing that may here befall,
For thou hast found all sovreignly
Of God a grace over others all.
In chastity of thy body
Conceive and bear a child thou shall.
This bidding bring I thee thereby –
His name Jesus shalt thou call.
Mickle of might then shall he be,
He shall be God, and called God's Son.
And David's seat, his father free,
Shall God give him to sit upon.
As king for ever reign shall he,
In Jacob's house for ever dwell;
Of his kingdom and dignity
Shall no man earthly know nor tell.

4. Then said the angel: Dread not thou, For ye be conceived with great virtue whose name shall be callèd Jesu; no-va, no-va. Nova, nova: AVE FIT EX EVA.

MARY: O thou God's angel meek and mild,
How should it be, I do thee pray,
That I should so conceive a child
Of any man by night or day?
I know no man that has defiled
My maidenhood, in sooth to say;
Without a will to workings wild,
In chastity have I been aye.

5. The Holy Ghost, God's spirit bright shall in great myst'ry on thee light, for thou art favoured in His sight; nova, nova. Nova, nova: AVE FIT EX EVA.

ANGEL: The Holy Ghost shall on thee light,
And over thee high virtue hold.
That holy birth of thine so bright,
The Son of God shall he be called.
Lo, 'Lizabeth thy cousin might
No child conceive, for she is old –
This is the sixth month now full right
To her that barren has been told.

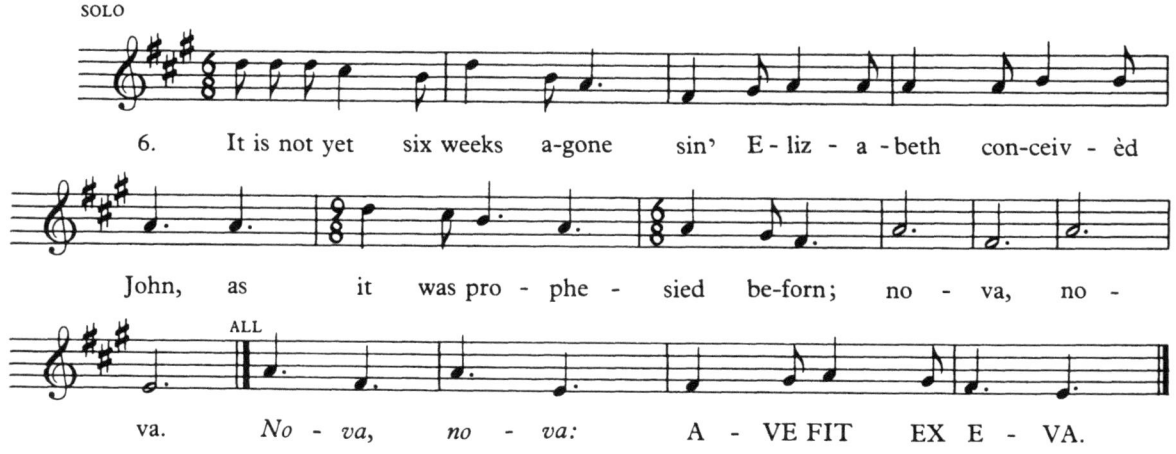

6. It is not yet six weeks agone sin' Elizabeth conceived John, as it was prophesied beforn; nova, nova. Nova, nova: AVE FIT EX EVA.

MARY: Thou angel, blessed messenger,
Of God's will do I hold me paid.
I love my Lord with heart full dear,
For grace that he has on me laid.
God's handmaiden, lo! I am here
To do his will all ready arrayd;
Be done to me in all manner
Through thy word even as thou hast said.

7. Then said the maiden: Verily, I am your servant right truly; Ecce ancilla Domini; nova, nova. *Nova, nova: A-VE FIT EX E-VA.*

ANGEL: Now God that all our hope is in,
Through might of Holy Ghost amain,
Save thee, lady, from stain of sin,
And guide thee from all workings vain.

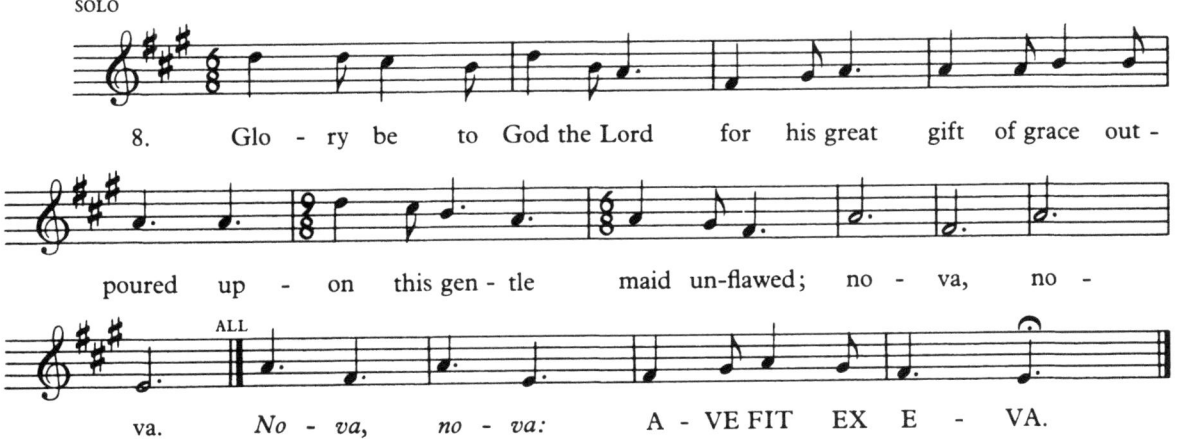

8. Glory be to God the Lord for his great gift of grace outpoured upon this gentle maid un-flawed; nova, nova. *Nova, nova: A-VE FIT EX E-VA.*

The words of the burden *Ave fit ex Eva* 'Ave is made from Eva' refer to the belief that the world is saved from the sin of Eve by the birth of Jesus, son of Mary ('Ave Maria' means 'Hail Mary'). 'Weened' means thought; 'y-wis' means certainly. Stanzas 5 and 8 are additions to the original carol.

# Part songs

## 4 *Two songs of praise*
### 4a *Nobilis, humilis*

Mighty Lord, gracious Lord, ever be Thy name adored!
Loving Lord, helpful Lord, grant us, by Thy grace restored,
Heaven's joy as our reward after earthly days.
Hear us sing in sweet accord songs of love and praise.

2  Every day, Lord, we pray: keep us in the heavenward way.
   Thus we pray day by day: never let us go astray.
   Make our lives, Lord, good and gay, purposeful and strong.
   Come to us and ever stay all the way along.

*Latin version*

Nobilis, humilis Magne, martyr stabilis,
Habilis, utilis Comes venerabilis
Et tutor laudabilis, Tuos subditos
Serva carnis fragilis Mole positos.

*Translation*

O virtuous, humble Magnus, steadfast martyr,
Capable, helpful, respected companion and praiseworthy guide,
Watch over your flock (who are) weighed down by the burden of their frail flesh.

This is the earliest known example of two-part music from the British Isles, and is of a kind known as *gymel,* in which the voices sing mainly a third (three notes) apart.

The original (Latin) text is a hymn to Magnus Erlendssohn (son of Erlin), patron saint of the Orkney Islands, who is said to have been murdered by his cousin Hakon (with whom he shared the rule) on the island of Egilsay in or about A.D.1116. The Cathedral at Kirkwall is named after him. St Magnus's day is 16 April.

*A stone carving of St Magnus*

## 4b *Edi beo thu*

2  As the sun arises in splendour,
   So you lighten earth's dark night.
   Out of you came forth a strong defender
   'Gainst the Devil's deadly might.
   None is there more truly near
   Although your glory shines afar.
   *My gracious lady, I pray you hear
   And bless me, lambent heav'nly star.*

*Alternative text (contrafactum)*

1. Welcome, haggard, staggering stranger,
   Gaunt of face and grim of eye!
   That you've experienced many a danger
   None who's seen you will deny.
   Scratched your hands and torn your cloak;
   I see a bandage encircling your head.
   And stains of blood have begun to soak
   Through, here and there, a dirty red.

2. Thanks to you, hospitable fellow,
   I shall soon be fit again.
   Grey is my hair which was once bright yellow,
   Through my suffering and pain.
   From the last crusade returned,
   I've fearful mem'ries of bloodshed and death,
   And dream again I see Athlit burned;
   I'll ne'er forget while I draw breath.

3. Take some courage, Templar tormented!
   Time will heal both flesh and mind.
   Here you'll find nightmares have all relented,
   Leaving troubles far behind.
   Then, when you're again quite well,
   I'll take you back to your homestead in peace
   Your farms to manage, your dreams dispel,
   Your tasks resume, your health increase.

Writing late in the twelfth century, the Welshman Gerald de Barri describes how ordinary folk in Wales and in the York area sang instinctively in harmony, a tradition which to a certain extent survives to this day. The simplest kind of improvised harmony – *gymel* – is exemplified in No. 4a. Naturally this very simple style began to develop more interesting features such as crossing of the parts, as in this example from a priory in Gloucestershire. Perhaps there is some Welsh influence in the piece, as Wales is certainly not far from Gloucestershire. Alternative words (a *contrafactum*) are provided in addition to the adaptation of part of the original Marian text. The piece was probably written some time in the 1260s. The lower part, which uses only three notes, may have been instrumental.

The village of Athlit was burned down in 1265 by Baybars, Mameluke Sultan of Egypt and Syria. The Knights Templars were a religious military order formed for the protection of pilgrims to the Holy Land. The order was suppressed in 1312.

*Seal of the Knights Templars*

# 5 Ad cantus laetitiae

2. Came an angel telling them
   They must go to Bethlehem,
   Town of David, Jesse's stem.
   *Alleluia!*

3. 'Hasten, hasten!' he did say,
   'Jesus Christ you'll find that way;
   Seek him out this very day.'
   *Alleluia!*

4. 'Sleeping in a manger bare
   'Neath his gentle mother's care
   Lies the Holy Child so fair.'
   *Alleluia!*

5. 'Glory be to God on high;
   Peace to mortal men be nigh.'
   Hear the host of angels cry.
   *Alleluia!*

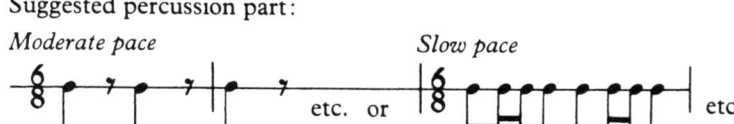

This short and simple two-part carol dates from the fourteenth century and was found in a library at Aosta, a cathedral town in north-west Italy.

Notice how the two voices exchange parts twice during the course of each stanza. This practice was not uncommon in medieval times. It has several advantages: there is less music to learn, the two parts are easier to sing together and both are of equal importance.

# 6 Two rondelli

*Rota* was the medieval term for what we call a round. The *rondellus* is similar, but differs from the *rota* in that the voices, instead of entering one after another with the same melody, start together, each at a different point in the same tune, the phrases of which each voice takes in a different order. Even so, a *rondellus can* be sung as a round, and these two are here arranged for that purpose.

## 6a *Alleluia*

No. 6a is a twelfth century *rondellus* from Barcelona in Spain. Its history is a little obscure; it was apparently found in a monastery in Catalonia by a Franciscan priest. The original text begins with the words '*crimina tollit*' – Latin for 'He bears (our) sins.' As notation in the twelfth century was not usually clear in showing the intended lengths of the notes and the rhythm of the music it is often possible to interpret the manuscript notes in a wide variety of rhythms. A selection of three possible solutions is given here; perhaps you can work out others for yourself.

## 6b *Rosa fragrans*

Keep us all from suf-fer-ing and sad-ness; Fill our hearts with joy and glad-ness; ⎯ Give us cha-ri-ty, hope and faith.

Optional percussion part (light):

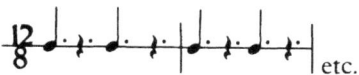

This is the first half of one of the *caudae*, or interludes, in a thirteenth century *conductus* found on a piece of manuscript in the binding of a book at Corpus Christi College, Oxford. The other half of the piece is rhythmically very different – and more difficult. The words ('O fragrant rose'), addressed to Mary, seem to have been written into the manuscript some time after the music. A *conductus* is a Latin song.

*A sixteenth-century musician as shown on a French tapestry*

# 7 Ave mater Domini

Walter Odington (who may have taken his name from a village in Gloucestershire) was a monk of Evesham in Worcestershire in the late thirteenth and early fourteenth centuries and wrote theoretical works on mathematics, astronomy and music. It is in the last-named that this *rondellus* (see No. 6) – presumably his own composition – appears. In the treatise it has no text except for the words *'Ave mater Domini'* ('Hail, mother of the Lord'), applied just to section D. The following plans give three suggested modes of performance: the first as a complete *rondellus*, and the second and third treating the two halves of the piece as independent rounds in their own right.

| | | | |
|---|---|---|---|
| Voice 3: | Plan 1: BCAEFD | Plan 2: – –ABC | Plan 3: – –DEF |
| Voice 2: | Plan 1: CABFDE | Plan 2: –ABCA | Plan 3: –DEFD |
| Voice 1: | Plan 1: ABCDEF | Plan 2: ABCAB | Plan 3: DEFDE |

# 8 Talent m'est pris

Suggested light percussion part (e.g., one tambourine):
*Moderately brisk pace*

A round is a form of canon, but a canon isn't always a round. As in a round, the performers of a canon all use the same tune, and each starts at a different time. But when a person taking part in the performance of a round reaches the end of his tune he can at once start again; this is not always the case with a canon. Many canons were composed in the fourteenth century, particularly in Italy and France. Some of them are very lively – and difficult to sing – and describe hunting scenes.

The call of the cuckoo has been imitated in music by composers from at least the thirteenth century to the twentieth, the most famous early example being *Sumer is icumen in*. The piece given here has been described by Rudolph von Ficker (in the *New Oxford history of music*, Vol. III) as 'the nearest French counterpart to the English *Sumer is icumen in*'. Although it is a canon it can be sung as a round, provided that the first note is halved in length (i.e. ♩.) on the second and subsequent occasions on which each voice part has the melody. The piece has been discovered in several manuscripts, and was therefore probably quite popular. In one source it is set to words by Oswald von Wolkenstein. The manuscript in which this version was found is from Ivrea, a cathedral town in north-west Italy, and was possibly used in the Papal court when the Pope lived in exile at Avignon. The 'cuckoo' sections of this canon use the device known as *hocket* (see No. 11b).

Don't be put off by a few discords in this piece – as long as they're the right ones! If you happen to know the famous round *Non nobis, Domine* you may notice that it starts in just the same way. The bracketed pause marks indicate suitable ending places for the three voice parts.

# 9 Two canonic songs

Some people would say that by the early sixteenth century the time of medieval music was well and truly past, and there is a good deal of truth in this. But in some countries (one of them England) the medieval spirit tended to linger on, and even the early Tudor composers Robert Fayrfax and William Cornyshe (c. 1465-1523) have a hint of the medieval about their music. For this reason – and because it is such a splendid piece – *Hey, Robyn* by Cornyshe has been included in this collection. Two voices sing in canon throughout while the third part represents a dialogue between two young men. This has led some editors to suggest that the third part is more effective divided between two groups of singers.

The composition comes from an early sixteenth century volume of music known as *Henry VIII's Book*. It contains over a hundred items of which nearly a third are by the King himself.

Plan of performance:
   Voice 1 sings ABABABA
   Voice 2 sings –ABABAB
   Voice 3 sings – –CDCEC
   If preferred, a fourth voice may sing E.

*King Henry VIII playing a harp to his jester*

# 9a Hey, Robyn

♩ = 108 (𝅗𝅥 = 54)

**A** Robin, hey! Robin, I say!

**B** Robin, hey! Robin, I say!

**C** Robin, hey! Robin, I say!

**D** My girl is pretty cool, I fear; I keep on wond'ring why. She / Tell me what your girl is like, and then we'll talk of mine.

**E** I can't believe that she would play a double game I find / That girls are true; my Jenny is a faithful one and kind.

(Inner voices:)
Tell me what your girl is like, and then we'll talk of mine.
Tell me what your girl is like, and then we'll talk of mine.
loves another fellow instead, or else she's very shy.

## 9b Martinslied

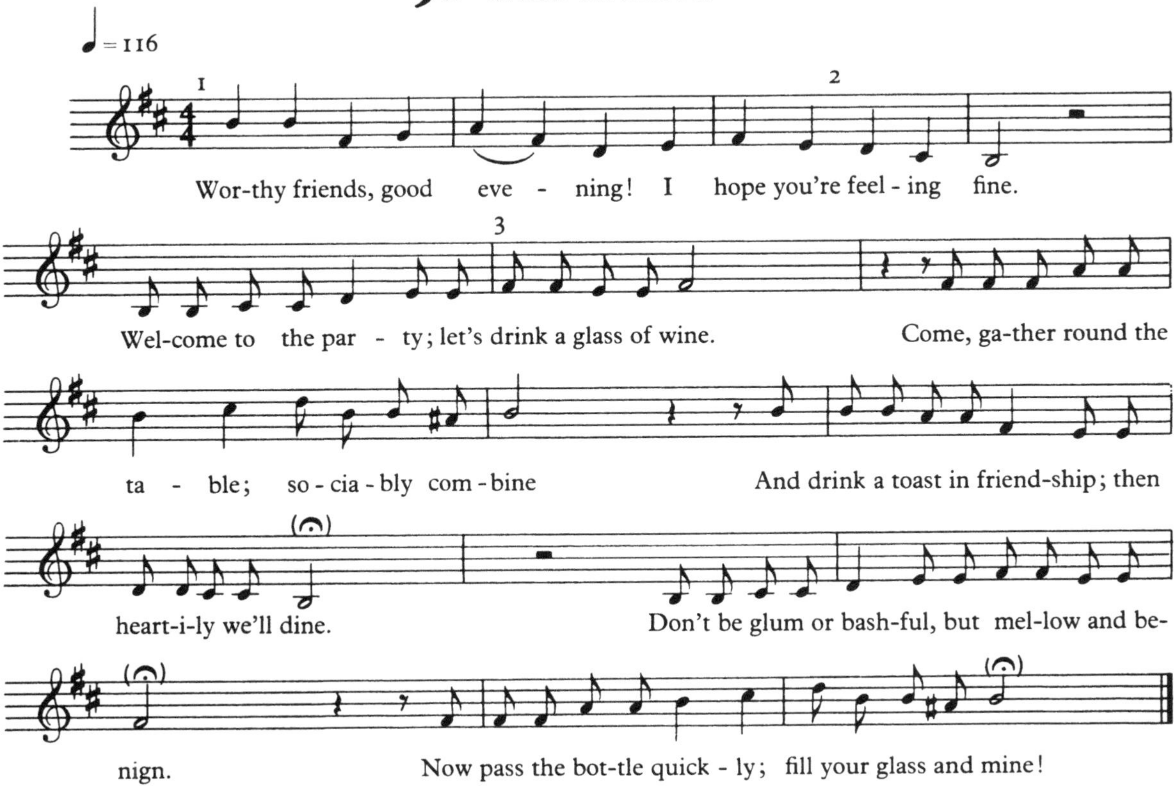

This three-part canon was found in a manuscript belonging to the monastery of Lambach in Germany. It was probably intended to celebrate Martinmas (11 November) and it sounds best sung by men's voices. It is not a round as we understand the term, so the second and third voices never reach the end. The drum part has been added in order to cover the startling lacunae or gaps which occur from time to time. But some people may like the slightly comical effect of the gaps, and so may prefer to leave out the drum part.

# Instrumental music

## 10 *Two instrumental dances*

Medieval music manuscripts which have no text under the notes may have been intended for instruments, but one can rarely be sure; the scribe may have forgotten to write in the words, or may have left the job to someone else who didn't do it. What is more certain is that much of the music was equally acceptable performed by voices or instruments. It's worth trying both.

One need have no hesitation about playing these tunes over and over again, varying the instrumental colour at each repeat or pair of repeats. No. 10b, for instance, may be played thirteen times without a break in a continuous build-up, thus: descant recorder alone; add tambourine; add tenor recorder; add triangle; add (tonic) drone; add tambour; add (dominant) drone; add glockenspiel; add drum; add clarinet (in its bottom octave); add (small) cymbals; add trumpet; add off-beat clapping.

*Early sixteenth-century French musicians – from a tapestry*

# 10a  *Danse royale (Ductia)*

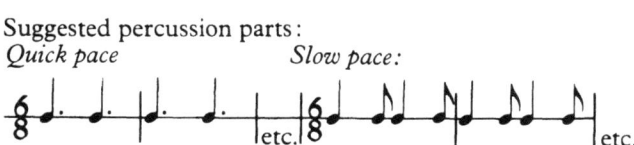

Suggested percussion parts:
Quick pace          Slow pace:

This is a French court dance of the thirteenth century; *ductia* is the name sometimes given to a short dance of the *estampie* type. THIS IS NOT A TWO-PART PIECE! Play either the upper or the lower notes according to preference; either line will suit the descant recorder. Treble recorders may perhaps read the lower part an octave higher.

## 10b *Ich spring an disem ringe*

Percussion parts as in (a) above.

Suggested drone:

This simple fifteenth-century song tune is very successful played repeatedly as a sprightly dance.

*Right: Fifteenth-century peasants dancing*

## 11 *Two vocal pieces for instruments*

In the thirteenth century a *conductus* was sometimes extended by a prelude, interlude and/or postlude – called a *cauda*, or tail – which had no words of its own. Some scholars believe (but others disagree) that these pieces were meant to be played on instruments, and they can certainly sound well so.

## 11a *Cauda*

Suggested percussion part:

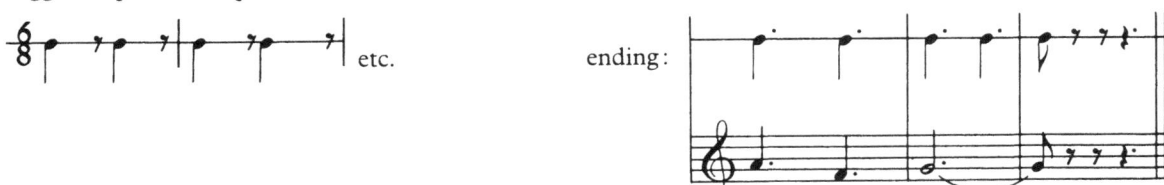

ending:

This piece comes from a manuscript written at St Andrews (Scotland) in about 1250. It may be played on recorders, flutes, oboes, violins, 'cellos (an octave lower) or even pitched percussion instruments, provided that both parts are played in the same octave.

## 11b *Amor potest*

Montpellier, a university town in the south of France, is about the size of Derby or Norwich. The medical school at Montpellier is housed in a former Benedictine monastery, home of one of the largest and most famous of all medieval music manuscripts, the Codex Montpellier. This contains 345 compositions, most of which are motets dating from the thirteenth century. The piece above, (Montpellier No. 328, which may be from the early fourteenth century) is interesting in several ways. The tenor (lowest) part repeats the same three notes over and over again (Denis Stevens, in the *Pelican history of music*, Vol. I, suggests that the part might be played on hand-bells) and, half-way through, the two upper parts begin to chase each other through a four-note figure. In some bars (25 and 30, for instance) there are examples of *hocket*, a medieval device in which voice parts sing alternately, one or two notes at a time, giving the effect of syncopation. The tenor part has no text (this is usual), nor even the customary word or two which would identify a plainsong origin, and the words of the upper parts stop half-way through, the rest of the piece being perhaps intended as a sort of vocal cadenza or *cauda*, after the fashion of No. 11a. So unless you feel like making up texts for the two upper parts (they were often different, and sometimes even in different languages) it will be best to treat the motet as an instrumental piece, either for descant recorders sounding an octave higher, for treble and tenor recorders, or a consort of suitable string and wind instruments sounding as written, or better still, an octave lower. Try to avoid a mixture of tone-colours in the same part. Relish the sturdy discordant 'crunches' between the upper parts; they are quite deliberate and all part of the fun.

*Musicians in procession, from an early sixteenth-century painting by Carpaccio*

## 12 Dit le bourguignon

It is very difficult to draw a dividing line in time between medieval and renaissance music, and of course opinions differ. John Dunstable, who was born about 1370, has been called a renaissance composer, and Robert Fayrfax, who lived until 1521, a medieval one. So we seem entitled to include this anonymous piece although it was published – in Venice – as late as 1501. As there is no text the music may be played by any reasonable combination of instruments, the most obvious being a consort of recorders: descant, treble, tenor and bass. Other instruments may be freely used, provided that (1) all play in the upper, or all in the lower, octave; (2) each part lies within the compass of the instrument concerned (essential, but easily overlooked!); (3) players of any transposing instruments used can either transpose their part as they play or write it out in a suitable key; and (4) viola players, if required and available, can read treble or bass clef parts. Remember also two important points: the descant recorder sounds an octave higher than written, and the trombone, though a non-transposing instrument when playing from bass or tenor clef, is often a transposing instrument when using the treble. The melody (third stave up or down) should be slightly prominent. The piece gains by being played with the notes detached, and not too quickly. Bar 19 of the top part may need a lot of practice! The word *bourguignon* means Burgundian.

# Suggestions for further activities

## Collections of music

Baines, Francis (ed.), *Dances from the Middle Ages*, London, Schott, 1965.

This is a collection of five pieces (six in fact, as one is in two contrasted sections) for descant or tenor recorder solo (or recorders in unison) with an added drum part. The music is useful and interesting for players with a fair degree of competence.

Dart, Thurston (ed.), *Invitation to medieval music*, 2 Vols. London, Stainer & Bell, 1967 and 1969.

Each of these two volumes contains a good graded selection of nineteen compositions for various combinations of voices and instruments by fifteenth-century musicians. The pieces represent a variety of subjects and styles, and range in standard from easy to fairly difficult, either technically or rhythmically. The song texts are the originals, and 'rough' translations are provided.

Davison, Archibald T., and Willi Apel (eds.), *Historical anthology of music*, Vol. 1. Cambridge, Massachusetts, Harvard University Press, rev. ed., 1949.

This invaluable collection of over 180 pieces covers the main streams of musical art from 1000 B.C. to the end of the sixteenth century. About fifty come under the medieval umbrella. Translations of the original texts and notes on each item are provided.

Dunston, Ralph, and Christopher Bygott, *Songs of the ages*, Huddersfield, Schofield & Sims, rev. ed., 1962.

The first edition (referred to in the Introduction to this collection) was called *Musical Appreciation through Song*. Admirable as it was as a work which pioneered the use of medieval music in schools, it suffered inevitably from the shortcomings of its time, and the 1962 revision by Frederick Westcott sets out to remedy those defects. The medieval section has been revised and expanded and the explanatory notes have been pruned and partly rewritten. The songs have English texts, though these may not all be to the taste of modern boys and girls. For those who want them, some of the piano accompaniments from the earlier edition have been retained.

Gennrich, Friedrich (ed.), *Troubadours, Trouvères, Minnesang and Meistergesang* Anthology of Music, Vol. 2, Köln, Arno Volk Verlag, 1960.

This volume contains some 78 medieval songs from France and Germany covering nearly 400 years, and is a happy hunting ground for anyone in search of practical material. A substantial introduction and commentary in English are provided, but there is no translation of the texts.

Gleason, Harold (ed.), *Examples of music before 1400*, New York, Appleton-Century-Crofts, 1942.

The book is an impressive selection of over a hundred pieces, ranging from Greek and Hebrew chants, through organum and secular monodic songs to motets, cacce and madrigals. Most of the old favourites are present, and although it is evident that much musicological water has flowed under the medieval bridge since the first appearance of the collection there is still a great deal to interest the seeker. The brief preface is of course in English, but the texts are all in the original languages.

Harrison, Frank Lloyd (ed.), *Now make we merthe*, 3 Vols. London O.U.P., 1968, *Two fourteenth-century carols*, London, Faber, 1968.

Between them the three slim books of *Now make we merthe* muster sixteen Christmas Carols dating from the twelfth to the sixteenth centuries, some for solo or unison voices and others polyphonic. In some cases instrumental accompaniments are provided, and the texts are translated into English at the end of each book. The carols have been recorded on Argo RG and ZRG 526. A very interesting and useful series, though rather expensive. The same comments apply to the *Two fourteenth-century carols*.

Husmann, Heinrich (ed.), *Medieval polyphony*, Anthology of Music, Vol. 9. Köln, Arno Volk Verlag, 1962.

This collection contains examples of organum, clausula, conductus, motet, caccia and madrigal, in from two to four voice parts. The introduction is in English, but the texts are all the originals. An interesting volume for the dedicated specialist, but its practical value for schools and amateurs is limited.

Ochs, Gerd (ed.), *Musik der Gotik*, Celle, Hermann Moeck Verlag, 1964.

This booklet of music for three recorders or other instruments contains six pieces covering a period of about 250 years from the time of the Notre Dame organa to that of Binchois. One of the items (the Machaut *Ballade*) does not go below (written) Middle C, and may therefore by played on three descant or tenor recorders, but the others need two descants and treble (the treble reading up an octave) or two tenors or flutes with violin or clarinet. Several of the pieces are rhythmically quite involved and may stretch – or even defeat – many an amateur musician.

Seagrave, Barbara G., and J. Wesley Thomas, *The songs of the Minnesingers*, Urbana, University of Illinois Press, 1966.

This is a substantial book (with an accompanying gramophone record) which gives valuable information on the Minnesingers, their background, their lives and their art, together with many examples of their songs. Both the original and English texts are provided. Expensive but very useful.

Thomson, John M. (ed.), *Early music*, London, Oxford University Press, 1973.

An enterprising quarterly periodical has been launched under this title. Its aim is 'to provide a link between the finest scholarship of our day and the amateur and professional listener and performer'. The adjective 'early' is interpreted liberally, and a wide range of topics is covered. The article in the first number (January 1973) on percussion instruments of the Middle Ages and Renaissance by James Blades is particularly valuable. Each issue contains a musical supplement in a practical edition.

Turner, Bruno (ed.), *Five thirteenth-century pieces*, London, Schott, 1962.

The first of these arrangements for three recorders needs a C instrument on its lowest part (unless a treble reads up an octave and plays with two descants), but the others may be played on 'equal' recorders, tenor, treble or descant, or by any convenient mixed combination, and the editor encourages the addition of string and percussion instruments. The parts are not difficult (the lowest – tenor – part is always easy, though low), but the hocket rhythm of No. 4 can raise problems.

There are also some useful medieval pieces in: Book 3 of Geoffrey Brace. *Something to sing.* Cambridge University Press, 1966.
McGrady, Richard J., *Four thirteenth-century pieces*, London, Chester, 1972 (for recorders).
Marr, Peter (ed.) *Four medieval pieces* (for) organ, London, Edition Peters, 1972.

The list of music sources below mentions some other collections.

## Background reading

Baines, Anthony (ed.). *Musical instruments through the ages*. Harmondsworth, Middlesex, Penguin Books, 1961.
Grout, Donald Jay. *A history of western music*. London, Dent, 1962.
Harman, Alec, Wilfrid Mellers and Anthony Milner. *Man and his music*. London, Barrie and Rockliff 1962.
Harrison, Frank Lloyd. *Music in medieval Britain*. London, Routledge and Kegan Paul, 1958.
Hughes, Dom Anselm (ed.). *New Oxford history of music*, vol. II. London, O.U.P., 1954.
Hughes, Dom Anselm and Gerald Abraham (eds.). *New Oxford history of music*, vol. III. London, O.U.P., 1960.
Reese, Gustave. *Music in the Middle Ages*. London, Dent, 1941.
Reese, Gustave. *Music in the Renaissance*. London, Dent, 1954.
Robertson, Alec and Denis Stevens. *Pelican history of music*, vol. I. Harmondsworth, Middlesex, Penguin Books, 1960.
Seay, Albert. *Music in the medieval world*. Englewood Cliffs, New Jersey, U.S.A., Prentice-Hall, 1965.
Smoldon, William L. *A history of music*. London, Herbert Jenkins, 1965.
Young, Percy M. *A history of British music*. London, Benn, 1967.

## Reference books

Apel, Willi (ed.). *The Harvard dictionary of music*. (see Editions, historical and elsewhere) London, Heinemann, 2nd ed., 1969.
Blom, Eric (ed.). *Grove's dictionary of music and musicians*. London, Macmillan, 1954.

The Bibliographies in *Man and his music*, *Music in the Middle Ages* and *New Oxford history of music* are useful.

## Records

The following records include songs from this book (indicated in parentheses). The list is not necessarily complete, and new recordings appear from time to time. Some of the records have now been deleted, but may occasionally be available second hand or from lending libraries.

*The central Middle Ages,* Archive APM 14018 (Nos. 2, 10a).
*Early music of England, Flanders, Germany and Spain,* Telefunken SAWT 9432-B (No. 10b).
*English medieval Christmas carols,* World Record Club SC 34 (No. 3).
*French court music of the thirteenth century,* Oiseau-Lyre SOL-R 332 (Nos. 10a, 11b).

*The history of music in sound*, H.M.V. HLP 4 (Nos. 6b, 11a).
*The medieval sound*, Oryx EXP 46 (No. 10a).
*Now make we merthe*, Argo RG 526 (No. 3).
*The play of Daniel*, Brunswick AXTL 1086/SXA 4001. From U.S.A.: DL79402 (No. 1).
*Secular music*, Telefunken SAWT 9504-A Ex (No. 2).
*Songs of love*, Abbey 604 (No. 9a).
*A tapestry of early Christmas carols*, Classics for Pleasure CFP 177 (No. 10a).

## Sources

English song words, except those in 2a, the six original stanzas of 3 and parts of 5, are by B. Sargent.

1. Music: Brit. Mus. Egerton MS 2615. Transcriptions in the editions of Noah Greenberg (1959), O.U.P. and William Smoldon (1960), Plainsong and Medieval Music Society. Original of No. 1a a tone lower, of No. 1b a perfect fourth higher and of No. 1c a tone lower. The text of the play is by W. H. Auden.
2. Music: Paris, Bibl. Nat. fr. 25566. Transcriptions of melodies in Gleason, *Examples of music 1400* and Axton & Stevens, *Medieval French plays* (1971), Blackwell. Original of No. 2a a perfect fourth higher and of No. 2b and No. 2c a tone lower. Words: R. Hague (slightly adapted).
3. Music: Glasgow, Hunterian MS 83. Transcription in J. Stevens (ed.), *Musica Britannica*, vol. IV (1958), Stainer & Bell. Original a minor third higher. Words of the carol: As for music. Play: Brit. Mus. Add. MS 35290. Edition by J. S. Purvis (1951), S.P.C.K.
4. Music: (a) Upsala C233, fo.19v-20; (b) Oxford, Corpus Christi College 59, fo.113. Transcription (a) Davison and Apel, *Historical anthology of music*, vol. I (1949), Harvard University Press, p. 22. (b) in *New Oxford history of music*, vol. II, p. 342.
5. Music: MS in the Library of the Seminary at Aosta. The transcription by Frank Harrison (*Two fourteenth-century carols*, 1968, Faber) is a tone lower and in 3/4 time, but is musically the same.
6. Music: (a) MS in a monastery in Catalonia; (b) Oxford, Corpus Christi College, 489, no.9. Transcriptions: (a) Wm. Tortolano (ed.), *Nineteen liturgical rounds* (1970), Gregorian Institute of America Publications; (b) *New Oxford history of music*, vol. II p. 376. Original pitch of (b) a perfect fourth higher.
7. Music: MS at Corpus Christi College, Cambridge, and C.E.H. de Coussemaker (ed.), *Scriptorum de musica medii aevi*, nova series 1864-76 Durand. Transcription in Gleason, *Examples of music before 1400*, p. 46. Original a perfect fourth higher.
8. Music: Ivrea MS, fo.52. Transcription in *New Oxford history of music*, vol. III, p. 136. Original a minor third higher.
9. Music: (a) Brit. Mus. Add. MS 31922; (b) Vienna, Nat. Bibliothek MS 4696. Transcriptions: (a) J. Stevens, *Musica Britannica*, vol. XVIII (1962), and G. Reese, *Music in the Renaissance* (1954), Dent, p. 770; (b) *Geschichte der deutschen Musik*, vol. I, p. 187. A different and shorter version of (b) appears in F. Jöde (ed.), *Der Kanon, Ein Singbuch für Alle*, vol. I, Möseler; and G. Brace, *Something to sing*, Book 3, C.U.P. Originals of both pieces a minor third higher.
10. (a) Paris, Bibl. Nat. MS Franç. 844; (b) *Lochamer (=Locheimer) Liederbuch*, c.1455, Berlin. Öff wiss Bibl. MS 40613. Transcription of (a) in P. Aubry (ed.), *Estampies et Danses Royales*, Librairie Fischbacher (1906). Also in F. Baines, *Dances from the Middle Ages* (1965), Schott & Co. Ltd. Originals of both pieces a tone lower.
11. (a) Wolfenbüttel MS 677 fo.54v; (b) Codex Montpellier, Fac. des Médecins H 196, fasc. VIII, fol.378v. Transcriptions: (a) *New Oxford history of music*, vol. II, p.334; (b) Y. Rokseth (ed.), *Polyphonies du XIIIe siècle* (1935- ), Editions de l'Oiseau Lyre.
12. *Harmonice Musices Odhecaton A* (Venice, Petrucci, 1501). Transcription in T. Dart, *Invitation to medieval music*, Book 2, (1969), Stainer & Bell, p.3. Original a tone lower.

## Sources of illustrations

**Front cover, pp. 1, 5** from Cantiga di S. Maria, Library of the Escorial, Madrid; **pp. 6 and 33** King Henry VIII's Psalter, The Trustees of the British Museum; **p. 7** Tenison Psalter, The Trustees of the British Museum; **p. 8** Mansell Collection; **p. 14** from A. Jeanroy, 'Le Chansonnier d'Arras', photograph Cambridge University Library; **p. 16** Bibliothèque Nationale Paris MS 77311, FR 25566; **p. 19** Bibliothèque Nationale Paris MS Fr 146 fo. 34r; **p. 25** Tankerness House Museum Kirkwall, photograph by D. B. Peace & Co.; **p. 27** The Trustees of the British Museum; **p. 30** Musee de Cluny, Paris, photograph by Giraudon; **p. 36** Paris, Mobilier national, private collection, photograph by Giraudon; **p. 38** Bibliothèque Nationale Paris MS Lat 1173 fo. 20v; **p. 42** Mansell Collection.

For EU product safety concerns, contact us at Calle de José Abascal, 56–1°, 28003 Madrid, Spain or eugpsr@cambridge.org.

www.ingramcontent.com/pod-product-compliance
Ingram Content Group UK Ltd.
Pitfield, Milton Keynes, MK11 3LW, UK
UKHW051918230326
469290UK00009B/158